At the Movies

Written by William O'Byrne

Contents	Page
Chapter 1. *Just Arrived!*	4
Chapter 2. *Theater Jobs*	6
Illustration Feature: *Preparing for a Movie*	14
Illustration Feature: *Filming a Movie*	16
Chapter 3. *A Movie-Making Journey*	18
Chapter 4. *Special Effects*	25
Photo Feature: *Special Effects Tricks*	28
Chapter 5. *Inside a Theater*	30
Index and Bookweb Links	32
Glossary	Inside Back Cover

Chapter Snapshots

1. Just Arrived! Page 4

Popcorn, ice cream, and video games! The fun of going to the movies starts as soon as you arrive at the theater!

2. Theater Jobs Page 6

With up to 6,000 people going to this theater each day, there are lots of jobs to do to make sure everyone enjoys their visit.

"But do you know what

3. A Movie-Making Journey Page 18

Who makes the movies we all enjoy? Come behind the scenes to find out about the different jobs that people do to make movies.

4. Special Effects Page 25

Sometimes the sounds you hear in a movie are not really what you think they are! Find out how coconut shells and chicken feathers help create some sound effects.

5. Inside a Theater Page 30

While we are enjoying a movie, it's nice to know we can feel safe, too.

happens behind the scenes ...?"

1. Just Arrived!

Sarah has just arrived at the theater with her sister, Penny. There's a delicious smell of popcorn coming from the concession stand. Sarah buys ice cream and Penny buys a box of popcorn.

When they turn around, they spot a separate candy counter. "Great!" That's their next stop.

At the candy counter, Sarah and Penny can't decide what candy to buy. Maybe they'll come back after the movie.

Sarah and Penny decide to sit with their uncle and watch the previews for new movies. He also gives them their tickets.

Just before the movie begins, their uncle allows them to play one game in the arcade. Lucky them!

But do you know what happens behind the scenes to bring you the movies you love to watch?

2. Theater Jobs

The Theater Manager

Richard is the manager of a theater complex. There are five movie theaters in his complex.

Richard wants everything to work just right at the theater so that people have a good time. Amongst his many jobs, he:
- chooses people to work in the theaters
- chooses films that people want to see
- makes sure the theater complex is safe
- makes sure that there is plenty of food and drinks

Advertising the Movies

Each morning, one of Richard's staff will update the movie screening times on the computer's answering machine. People can telephone the theater and hear what movies are playing and when they will be shown. Every week, Richard places advertisements for the movies in the newspapers. Sometimes he will also advertise the movies on the radio.

The Theater Workers

Most of the people who work at the theater complex are high school or college students. Each student learns about all of the jobs. They learn how to sell tickets, work in the concession stand, and become an usher.

The best part of their jobs is being able to see the movies for free!

The Concession Stand Workers

Will is one of the part-time theater workers. At other times, he is a college student.

Will's main job is to work in the concession stand. Sometimes, on a very busy night, he sells the tickets, too. Imagine selling tickets, ice cream, and drinks — all at the same time! Will says it can get a bit *too* busy!

When it's really busy, up to 6,000 people a day will go to the theater complex.

On busy days, concession stand workers can sell up to 4,000 candy bars and thousands of drinks.

In one day, up to 60 pounds of popcorn can be sold — enough to fill a small room!

What Is Popcorn?

Popcorn is a snack food that is made from grains of corn. The grains of corn are picked when they are very young, and the corn kernels are very small. If the corn was left to grow, it would become sweet corn!

The grains of corn are heated until they burst — this is why they are called "popcorn"! When they burst, they become fluffy, light, and very yummy to eat.

The Ushers

Ushers check people's tickets before they go into the theater to watch the movie. When people are late, ushers may show them to empty seats.

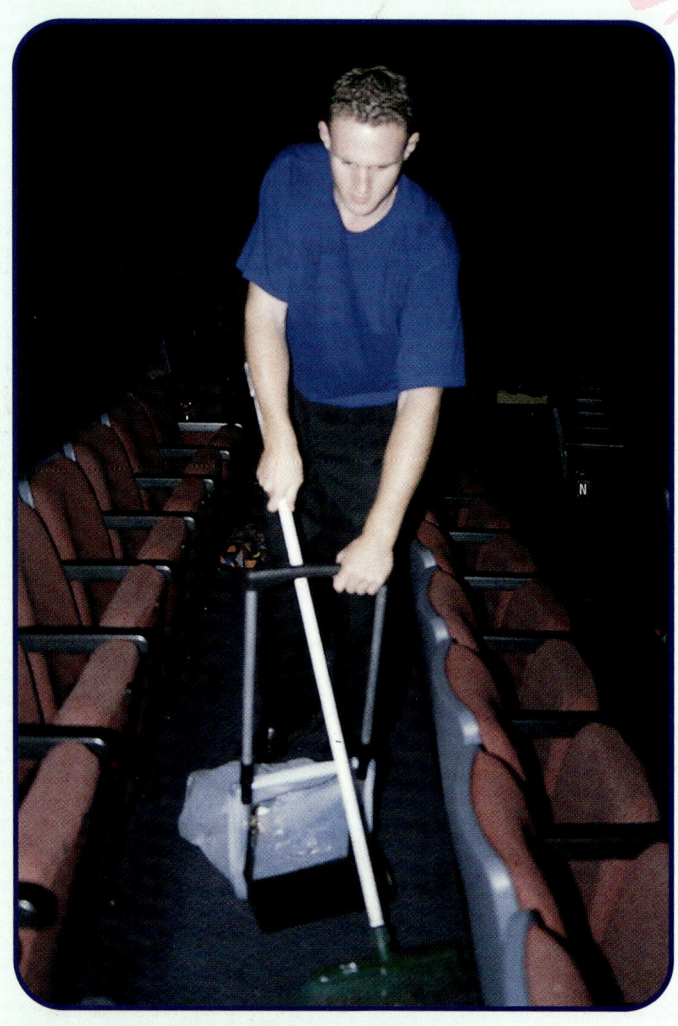

An usher cleans between the seats.

When each movie is finished, Richard's ushers clean up the trash. They're happiest when people use the trash cans. They're the unhappiest when people leave garbage at their seats!

The theaters must be cleaned before people are let in for the next movie.

The Projectionists

David and Paul are projectionists. They like being projectionists because it is an interesting and responsible job. If they are not careful, people won't enjoy the movie. Who wants to watch a blurry movie? And who wants to listen to sound that is too low or too loud?

Paul adjusts the sound levels for a movie on the theater's sound system.

While the movies are being shown, David and Paul check each film two or three times. What are the two worst problems?

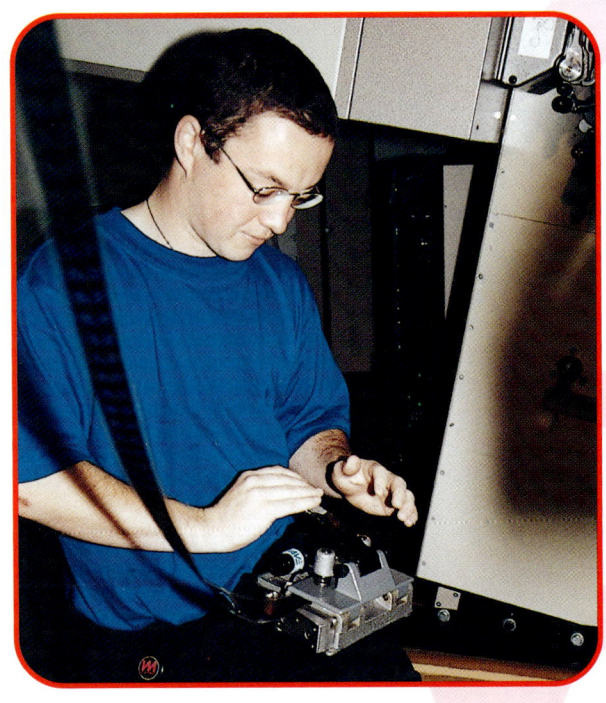

First, the film can break. If it does, David will splice, or join, the two ends of the film together.

David uses a special machine to splice the two ends of the film together by overlapping them.

Metal Platters

Film reels are so long, they are placed on large metal trays, called platters. The platters help the films run smoothly.

The second worst problem is that the powerful bulb in the projector can blow up. One of the most important parts of the projector is the bulb.

Graham helps out by replacing the xenon bulb in the projector. He is the theater's Technical Manager.

Powerful Light Bulbs

The xenon bulbs in a projector are very bright. They take a small image off the film and enlarge it to 18 yards wide on the screen. They put out 1,000 watts of power. Most light bulbs in your house put out between 60 to 100 watts of power.

3. A Movie-Making Journey

How Are Movies Made?

Many people are needed to make a movie. There are also many stages in making a movie. Follow our six stages in a movie-making journey.

STAGE 1: THE MOVIE SCRIPT

The **screenwriter** writes the screenplay. It is a story about what will happen in the movie's scenes. The story must have a beginning, a middle, and an ending. This is what a screenwriter might write about a dinosaur scene.

> A dinosaur is angry. It is chasing a mother and her son toward their car.

The **writer** writes the movie script. First, the writer reads the screenwriter's screenplay. Then the writer writes more ideas and creates interesting characters. The writer may also work on the script with other writers. This is what a writer could write for the same dinosaur scene.

THE DINOSAUR (roars loudly)
THE SON (shouting) "Mom! It's going to catch us!"
THE MOTHER (shouting and pushing her son toward the car) "Hurry! Let's get in the car!"

STAGE 2: PREPARING FOR THE MOVIE

The **producer** reads the screenplay and the movie script. If the producer likes the ideas for the movie, he or she organizes the money to pay for the movie to be made.

The **director** decides how the film will be made, and works closely with the producer. Then the director works with the writer to find out more about the scenes and the characters. The director draws sketches for each scene and plans the best way to film the movie.

The **casting agent** chooses the best **actors** to perform each of the characters' roles.

The **art director** designs the sets, costumes, and props needed to make the actors and the scenes in the movie look their best.

STAGE 3: FILMING THE MOVIE

The **director of photography** films each scene with **camera** and **lighting operators**. They film the actors either inside a studio on different sets, or outside on location, such as a beach.

The director works with the director of photography and the actors to make the best movie for people to enjoy.

There may be hundreds of people in the **film crew** who also work on making the movie. At the end of a movie, you can read a list of the film crew's names. The list is called "the credits."

STAGE 4: FINISHING THE MOVIE

The **sound editor** mixes many sounds together for the movie. The sound editor may mix sounds from four sound tracks: the actors' voices, the sound effects, the music, and the background sounds.

The **film editor** decides which parts of the film should be in the movie. The director and the film editor may work together to decide the order of each scene or part. They may end up looking at hundreds of hours of film.

Once the producer and the team are happy with the movie, it is sent to the **film distributor**.

Movie Sound Tracks

The movie sound track includes all the speaking parts, music, and sound effects. Some movies have their sound tracks on the film's reel. Other movies have their sound tracks on CDs that are played at the same time as the movie is shown.

STAGE 5: DISTRIBUTING THE MOVIE

The film distributor buys movies to show in theaters or on television around the world. It is their job to advertise the movies and to send trailers, or previews, to theaters.

There are many film distribution companies around the world. They rent out films, just like video stores do. But their customers are movie theaters. They are paid some of the money that theaters make from selling tickets.

Trailers

Trailers show you parts of a movie. A clever trailer excites you about the movie without letting you know too much about the story, or plot.

STAGE 6: THE MONEY!

Once the movie is finished, everyone who worked on it is paid! What happens if a lot more people go to see the movie than the producer expected? Some of the people associated with the movie get even *more* money later!

Film Classification

Before a film can be shown in theaters, it is given a rating. That way, people know what age you need to be to see the film. The five main ratings are:

G — General	Can be seen by people of all ages.
PG — Parental Guidance	May be suitable for children under the age of 13 years (only if the parents approve).
PG–13 — Mature	For people over the age of 13 years.
R — Restricted	Can only be seen by adults who are 18 years and older.

Video and Television Distribution

After movies are shown in the theaters, they can be distributed to video stores, and later sold to television networks. Usually movies are available on video six months after they were first shown in theaters. After that, the same movies can be seen about two years later on television.

4. Special Effects

Special effects are what we *see* in the movies. Sound effects are the special sounds that we *hear* in the movies.

Sound Effects

If someone is being filmed walking down the street, there are many background sounds. You may hear cars, birds, footsteps, and even the sound of the camera being wheeled along beside them. If you heard these sounds in a movie, it would be very noisy! So movie-makers film the scenes with no background sounds. Later, they record the sounds separately.

With all these people needed to make a movie, it can get very noisy in the background!

The movie's sounds are recorded in a quiet studio by a "foley artist." Gerry is a foley artist. He works in a huge room that is like a noise-making playground — full of all sorts of junk! In this room are a lot of pits with lids. Underneath the lids are different surfaces such as concrete, sand, wood, and pebbles.

To make the sound of footsteps for a movie, Gerry walks on the correct surface. A microphone records the sound of his feet moving up and down in time with the actor in the film. Simple!

Sounds	How the Sounds Are Made
Leaves rustling in the wind	Shake a leafy branch.
Creaky/spooky sounds	Scrunch a leather jacket.
Jingling sounds (e.g., keys)	Shake dog collars, spurs, and bridles.
Birds flying	Chicken feathers are stuck together like wings and waved in the air.
A duck walking	A pair of swimming flippers are "walked" on the floor.
A horse walking	A coconut shell cut in half is "walked" on the floor.
Squishy/blood-thirsty sounds	Tomatoes and watermelons are squashed.

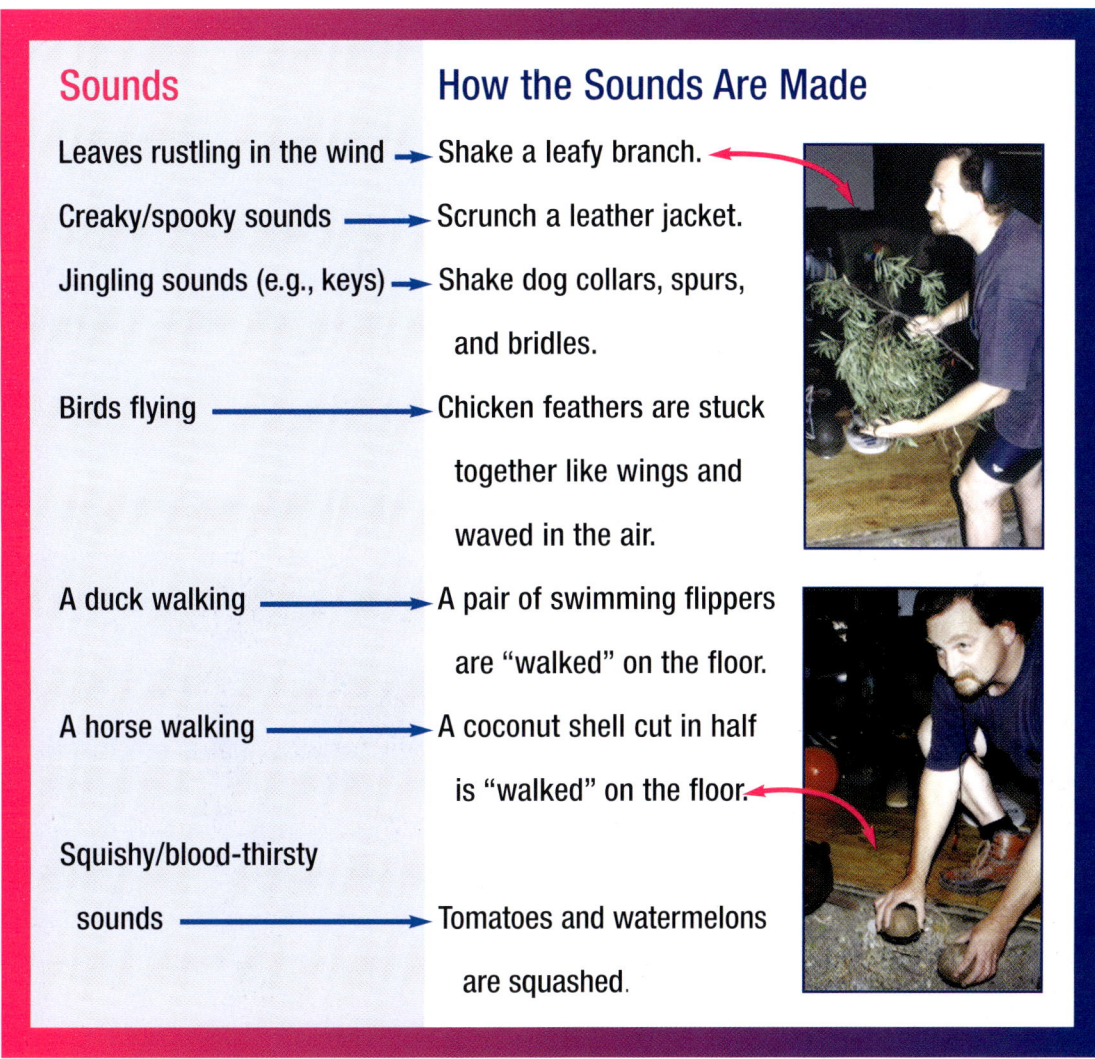

Sometimes a foley artist combines different sounds to make one BIG sound. Here's an example:

1. Hit a leather jacket
2. Snap a piece of wood
3. Twist a bunch of celery

Sounds **1 + 2 + 3 = A BIG NASTY PUNCH!**

Special Effects Tricks

Special effects have been used in movies for some time. Many types of special effect tricks have been created.

Images can be created using high-tech computers. Once an image is created it can be combined with other images. These computers can make almost anything imaginable in movies.

Made-up pictures can be produced that seem real on the movie screen. Sometimes miniature models are built. They are much less expensive to use, and on film, they look the actual size.

Movie crew members use a dust machine to create strong winds and blow the sand.

5. Inside a Theater

Inside theaters, people's safety is very important. If the fire alarm sounds, or there is another emergency, the ushers will help people move safely outside. There are plenty of exits to get out of the theaters quickly.

The ushers tell people not to run or push. That way, everyone gets out sooner and safely.

Theater Speakers

Many theaters have "surround sound." This means they have four sets of speakers. In the center of the theater are the speakers for dialogue (speech). At the right and left side of the theater are the speakers for most of the music and the background sounds. At the back of the theater are the speakers for sound effects.

*The screen is dark,
the seats are full,
The movie's
about to begin!*

*The action's great!
The music's loud!
And the goodies
will always win!*

The First Films

The first films were called "silent pictures," because people didn't know how to add sound to the movie. In many silent films, the actor's words were shown at the bottom of the screen.

Feature Films

The first feature film made in America was "Oliver Twist" in May 1912. The first feature film lasting longer than one hour was "The Story of the Kelly Gang." It was made in Australia in 1906. The first feature film made in England was "Oliver Twist" in August 1912.

Index

advertisements 7, 23
art director 21
casting agent 20
CDs 22
classification 24
computer 7
director 20, 21, 22
director of photography 21
distribution 23, 24
film crew 21
film distributor 23
film editor 22
film reels 12, 22
foley artist 26
games 2, 5
ice cream 2, 4, 8, 9
Imax 28
light bulbs 13
microphone 26
popcorn 2, 4, 9
producer 20, 22, 23
projectionists 11–12
safety 30
screenwriter 18
screens 28
sound editor 22
sound effects 3, 22, 25–27, 30
sound levels 11
sound tracks 22
speakers 30
theater workers 7–13
tickets 8, 23
trailers 5, 23
writer 19, 20

Bookweb Links

Read more Bookweb 3 books about movies:

I Spy! — Nonfiction
Starstruck! — Fiction

Key To Bookweb Fact Boxes
☐ Arts
☐ Health
☐ Science
☐ Social Studies
☐ Technology